When Get Angry

Dr. Warren Heydenberk
&
Dr. Roberta Heydenberk

PublishAmerica
Baltimore

© 2000 by Warren and Roberta Heydenberk.
All rights reserved. No part of this book may be reproduced in any form without written permission from the publishers, except by a reviewer who may quote brief passages in a review to be printed in a newspaper or magazine.

First printing

ISBN: 1-58851-354-8
PUBLISHED BY PUBLISHAMERICA, LLLP
www.publishamerica.com
Baltimore

Printed in the United States of America

Praise for
When I Get Angry

"In our family, we tell our children that it's okay to get angry. It's how you deal with the anger that counts. The Heydenberks' new book, When I Get Angry, helps kids realize that they have choices. As a parent, this is the kind of book I have waited for, and one my kids enjoy too." Brian S. Conklin, Executive Director, The Peace Center, 102 West Maple Ave., Langhorne, PA

* * * * *

" Students who learn how to manage their anger in their youth will reap lifelong rewards. When I Get Angry gives students the skills they need to manage their anger in a peaceful and successful way." M. Jane Nace, M.Ed., School Counselor, Quakertown School District, Quakertown, PA

* * * * *

"When I Get Angry rhymes and it's funny. This makes it easy to talk to your children about this important subject." Judith Scheetz, parent, Applebachsville, PA

Dedicated to our *When I Get Angry* actors: Adam, Alecia, Anna, Corrine, Ethan, Isaac, Isabella, Jake, Justin, Linda, Madison, Mikaela, Robert, Ryan, and Sebastian.

When I get angry I…

Hide in a closet and wring my hands
Because no one ever understands.

And then...

My friends run away and shut the door
So they won't hear me anymore.

When I get angry I...

Run in the yard or go for a walk
Until I'm calm enough to talk.

And then…

I sit down with my friends and work it out
Because that's what friendship is all about.

When I get angry I...

Hug my dog for a minute or two
And try to imagine a new point of view.

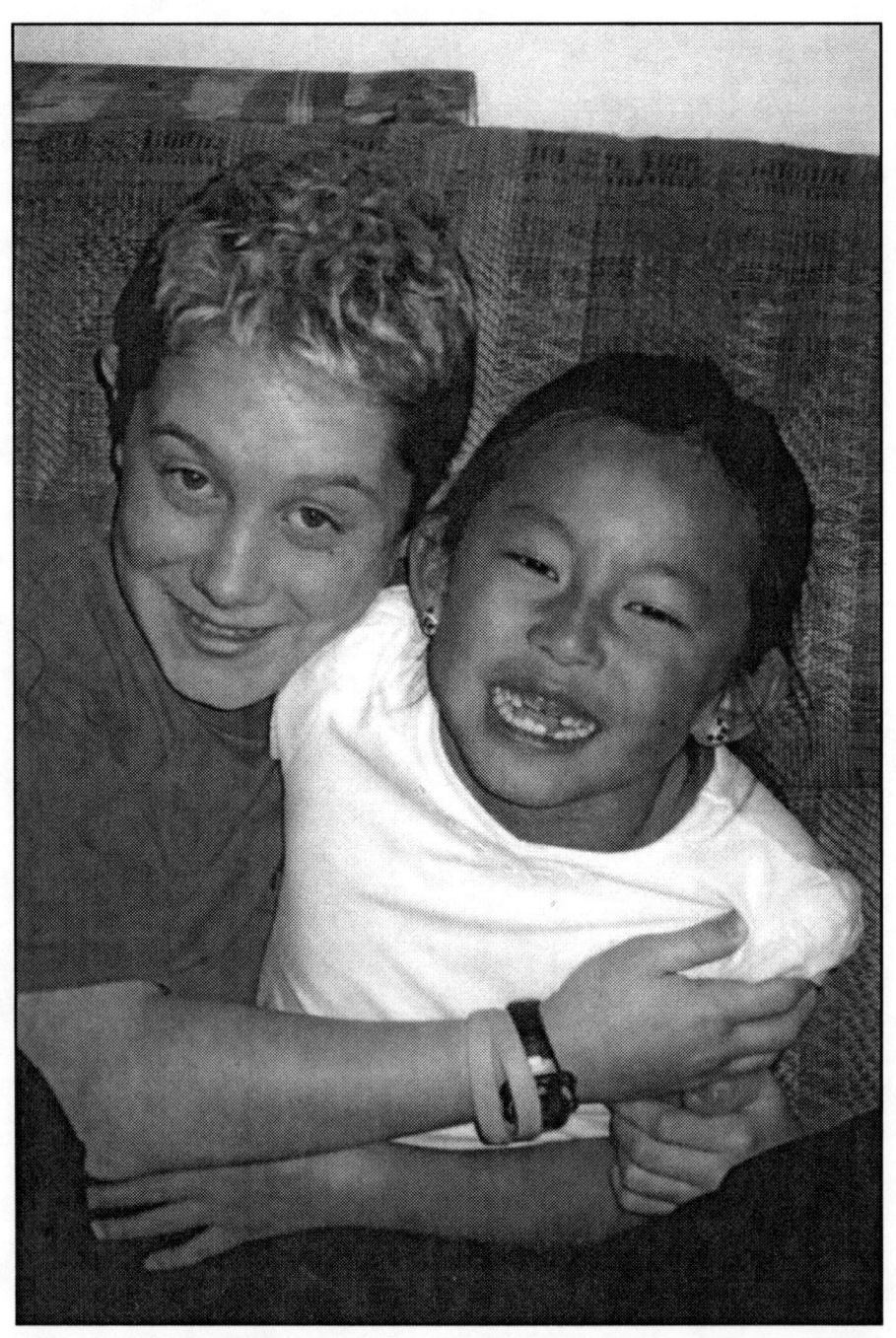

And then...

I sit down with my friends and work it out
Because that's what friendship is all about.

When I get angry I…

Bark and howl and roar and moo
And act like an animal at the zoo.

And then…

My friends run away and shut the door
So they won't hear me anymore.

When I get angry I…

Stop before I raise my voice
And try to make a better choice.

And then…

I sit down with my friends and work it out
Because that's what friendship is all about.

When I get angry I…

Scream and yell and point and blame
And call my friend a nasty name.

And then…

My friends run away and shut the door
So they won't hear me anymore.

When I get angry I…

Make my favorite thing to eat
And give myself a calm-down treat.

And then…

I sit down with my friends and work it out
Because that's what friendship is all about.

When I get angry I…

Write a poem or sing a song
About what happened and what went wrong.

And then…

I sit down with my friends and work it out
Because that's what friendship is all about.

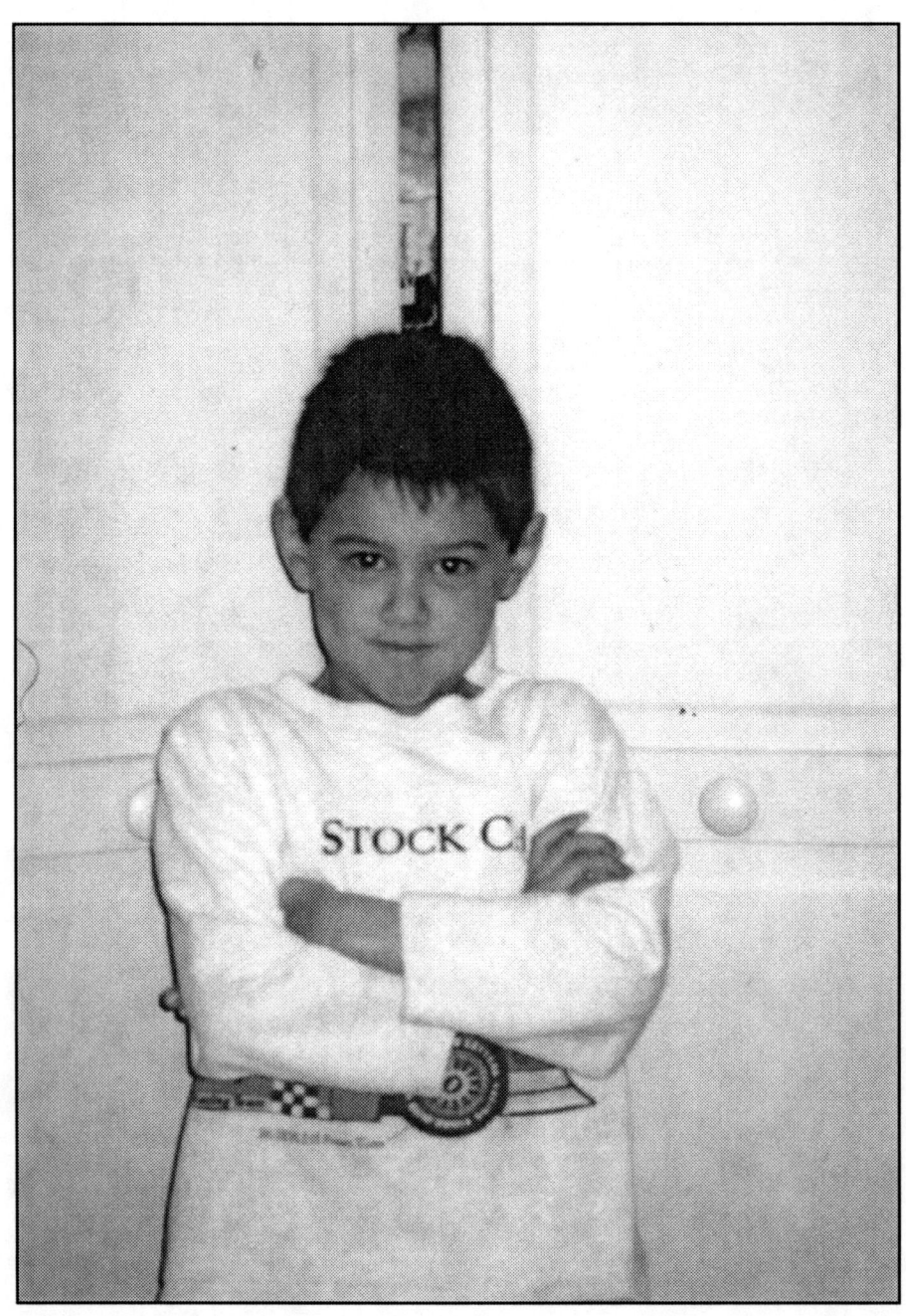

When I get angry I…

Whine and blame and fume and steam until
Everyone else gets angry and mean.

And then…

My friends run away and shut the door
So they won't hear me anymore.

When I get angry I…

Take a deep breath and count to ten
And wait until I can think again.

And then…

I sit down with my friends and work it out
Because that's what friendship is all about.

When I get angry I…

Take a deep breath and count to twenty
And try to think of something funny.

And then…

I sit down with my friends and work it out
Because that's what friendship is all about.

When I get angry I…

Jump up and down
And act like a clown.

And then…

My friends run away and shut the door
So they won't hear me anymore.

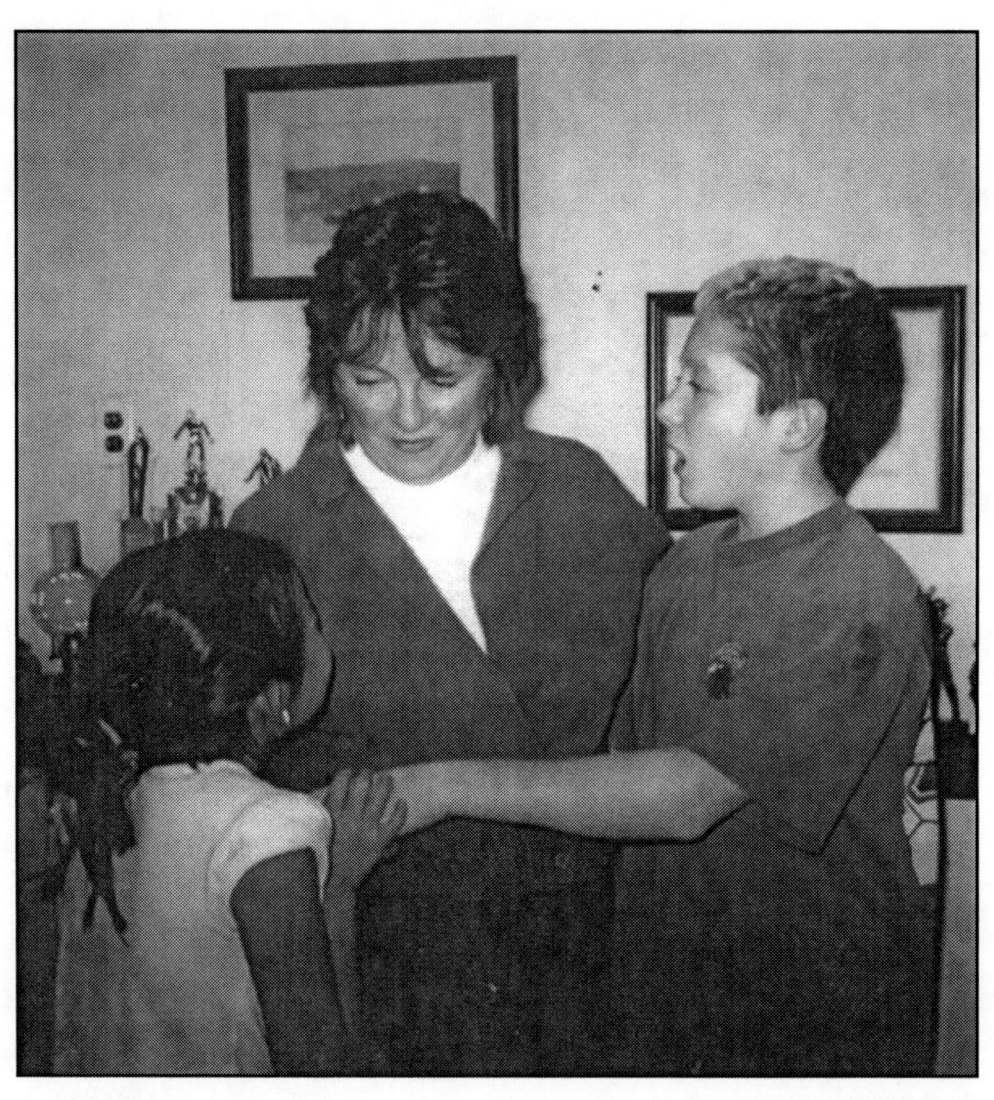

When I get angry I…

Talk to my mom about how I'm feeling
Before I explode and hit the ceiling.

And then…

I sit down with my friends and work it out
Because that's what friendship is all about.

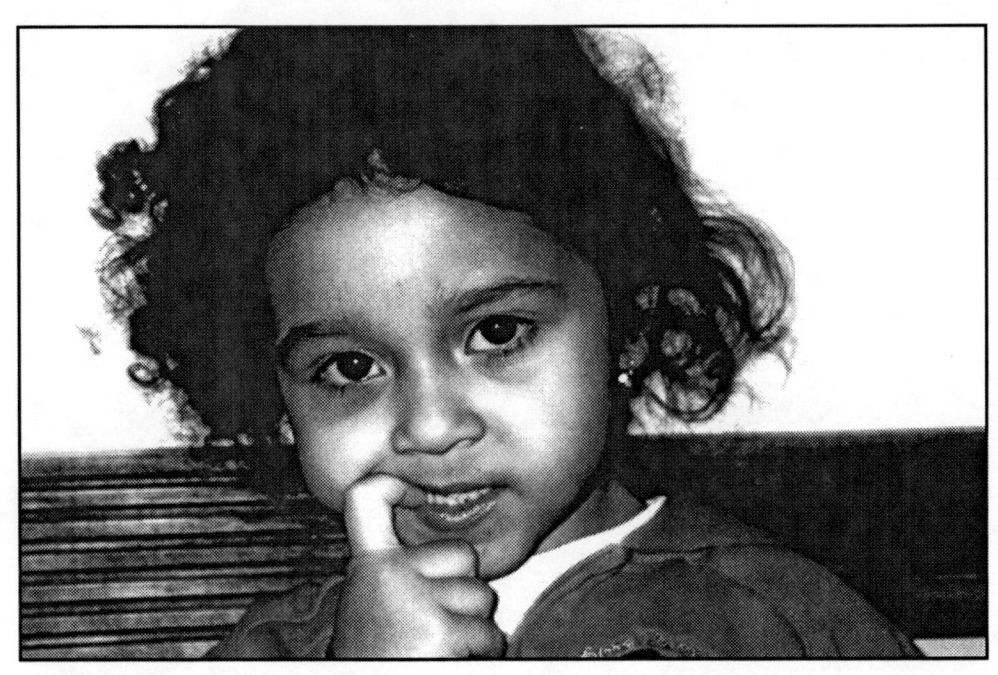

When I get angry I…

Ask myself the kind of questions
That turn my problems into lessons.

And then…

I sit down with my friends and work it out
Because that's what friendship is all about.

What do you do when you get angry?

And then what happens?

Here are the five steps that super problem solvers use:

Step 1—STOP

**It's OK to feel angry,
But don't do anything to make it worse.
Take a break and calm down for a minute first.**

Step 2—UNDERSTAND

**Ask yourself, "How do I feel?"
"Why do I feel this way?"
"How do other people feel about this?"**

Step 3—THINK

Think of ways to make the problem better.
Ask yourself, "What can I do to make this better?"
Ask your friend what he/she thinks.
Get as many ideas as you can.

Step 4—CHOOSE

Pick the best idea or plan to solve the problem.
Try to choose a plan that makes everyone happy.

Step 5—TRY THE PLAN

Try the plan that you chose.
If it doesn't work, go back to Step 3 (THINK).
Find another way to solve the problem.

Printed in the United States
91552LV00003B/379-411/A